Dian Fossey

Heidi Moore

Raintree

Chicago, Illinois

HEINEMANN-RAINTREE

TO ORDER:

☎ Phone Customer Service **888-454-2279**

💻 Visit **www.heinemannraintree.com** to browse our catalog and order online.

Editorial: Louise Galpine, Rachel Howells, and Adam Miller
Design: Kimberly R. Miracle and Betsy Wernert
Illustrations: Mapping Specialists, Inc.
Picture Research: Mica Brancic and Helen O'Reilly
Production: Vicki Fitzgerald

Originated by Modern Age
Printed and bound in China by Leo Paper Group.

ISBN-13: 978-1-4109-3225-9 (hc)
ISBN-10: 1-4109-3225-7 (hc)

13 12 11 10 09
10 9 8 7 6 5 4 3 2 1

Library of Congress Cataloging-in-Publication Data
Moore, Heidi, 1976-
  Dian Fossey / Heidi Moore.
     p. cm. -- (Great naturalists)
  Includes bibliographical references and index.
  ISBN 978-1-4109-3225-9 (hc)
  1. Fossey, Dian--Juvenile literature. 2. Primatologists--United States--Biography--Juvenile literature. 3. Gorilla--Rwanda--Juvenile literature. I. Title.
  QL31.F65M66 2008
  599.884092--dc22
  [B]
                                    2007049820

Acknowledgments
The author and publisher are grateful to the following for permission to reproduce copyright material: © Ardea p. **26** (Chriss Martin Bahr); © Corbis pp. **5**, **37**, **38** (Yann Arthus-Bertrand), **9** (Joanna Vestey), **11** (Bettmann), **27**, **31** (Paul Souders), **13** (Staffan Widstrand), **14**, **17** (Andy Rouse); © Dian Fossey Gorilla Fund International pp. **4**, **6**, **32**, p. **41** (Peter G. Velt); © Getty Images pp. **39** (Minden Pictures/Ingo Arndt), **40** (Nicholas Kamm/©2005 AFP); © Last Refuge p. **34** (Adrian Warren); © National Geographic Society p. **20**, **23**, pp. **15** (Van Lawick Hugo), pp. **18-19**, **21-22**, **24-25**, **30**, **33**, **36** (Robert Campbell); © Nature Picture Library p. **25** (Richard du Toit), pp. **28**, **35** (Bruce Davidson); © RKO p. **29** (The Kobal Collection).

Cover photograph of Dian Fossey reproduced with permission of ©Getty Images (Time Life Pictures/Neil Selkirk).

The publishers would like to thank Nancy Harris for her assistance in the preparation of this book.

Every effort has been made to contact copyright holders of any material reproduced in this book. Any omissions will be rectified in subsequent printings if notice is given to the publisher.

CONTENTS

Some words are shown in bold, **like this**. You can find out what they mean by looking in the glossary.

HOME AMONG THE GORILLAS

The mist rises in the densely forested mountains of central Africa. A group of 11 gorillas rests near a cluster of tall trees in a meadow. The youngest clings to its mother's chest.

Suddenly the oldest male, the **silverback**, hears a noise. Could it be a hunter? Or a male gorilla from another group? Sensing danger, the animal pounds his muscular chest. This sends a warning to the visitor to leave the group alone.

Mountain gorillas live in the forests of central Africa. This female gorilla is pictured with her baby in Virunga National Park, Rwanda.

Watching the apes

Someone is crouched in the trees, quietly watching the group. This visitor to the forest is Dian Fossey, a U.S. naturalist. A naturalist is someone who studies nature and living things. Fossey spent nearly 20 years living in **remote**, or hard to reach, areas of Africa to study rare mountain gorillas.

All about gorillas

Gorillas are not fierce animals. They are usually shy, though they may strike out if they feel threatened. At times they show curiosity, especially when visitors, such as humans, enter their **habitat**. They do not often approach visitors, but instead watch them from a safe distance.

Dian Fossey dedicated her life to studying mountain gorillas.

Gorillas are humans' closest relatives after chimpanzees. But before Fossey's work with mountain gorillas in the wild, people knew very little about them.

Fossey watched gorillas closely for many years. She learned about their family groups, their behaviors, and their diet. She learned how to tell them apart. Over time she came to know each gorilla like a family member or a friend. She fought fiercely to protect the gorillas she loved so much. Because of Fossey's curiosity, patience, and careful research, we now know far more about mountain gorillas than ever before.

"I have made my home among the mountain gorillas."

Fossey wrote this in her famous book, *Gorillas in the Mist.*

Naturalist in Training

Dian Fossey was born in San Francisco, California, on January 16, 1932. She was the only child of George and Kitty Fossey.

Dian said that she had a difficult childhood. Her parents separated when she was young. She did not see her father for many years. Eventually her mother remarried. Her mother and new stepfather had many rules.

As a child, Dian loved animals, especially horses. She had a goldfish for a short time until it died. She also took horseback-riding lessons.

Even as a child Dian had a keen interest in animals.

Ranch hand

When Dian Fossey was 19 years old, she worked as a ranch hand in Montana. A ranch is a type of farm in the western United States where people raise animals. A ranch hand takes care of the animals. Dian loved doing this. But she came down with chickenpox and had to go back to California early.

Growing up

Dian graduated from Lowell High School, in San Franciso, in 1949. Then she went off to college. First she attended Marin Junior College, taking business classes. She did not like her course and switched to the University of California at Davis. She wanted to become a **veterinarian**. Veterinarians, or vets, are doctors who take care of animals. This was a good fit because Dian loved animals. But she struggled with some of her classes.

After two years she switched to San Jose State. She graduated in 1954 with a degree in **occupational therapy**. Occupational therapists help sick and injured people relearn daily tasks, such as dressing, eating, and performing a job.

Early career

When she was 23 Dian Fossey moved to Louisville, Kentucky. She took a job as an occupational therapist at Kosair Children's Hospital. There she helped injured, sick, and **disabled** children perform daily tasks.

For ten years Fossey lived on a farm and worked at the hospital. The work was challenging but rewarding. She enjoyed helping her patients, but she also dreamed of exploring the world. Then she read U.S. naturalist George Schaller's study of rare mountain gorillas. The book made her want to see them for herself. She did not know at the time that the skills she had gained working with children would help her during her time in Africa with the mountain gorillas. Working with children had given her patience and persistence, or the ability to stick with things without giving up.

Leaving the farm

Fossey wrote in her book *Gorillas in the Mist*, "I spent many years longing to go to Africa because of what that continent offered in its wilderness and great diversity of free-living animals. Finally I realized that dreams seldom materialize on their own."

Fossey decided to travel to Africa on a **safari**. She would take a journey to observe wild animals up close. She hoped to catch a glimpse of the mountain gorilla! She planned her trip for months and took out a bank loan to pay for it.

First among the mountain gorillas

George Schaller was the first person to study mountain gorillas in the wild. He spent two years observing the gorillas in central Africa. His book *The Mountain Gorilla: Ecology and Behavior* was published in 1963. Until Fossey studied the gorillas, most of what people knew about them came from Schaller's work.

Naturalist George Schaller's work inspired Dian Fossey. He is pictured here in Central Park Zoo, New York.

African safari

Fossey prepared for her journey to Africa. She wrote to a safari company in Nairobi, Kenya, and hired a driver for the trip. When she arrived, the driver would take her to different parts of Africa.

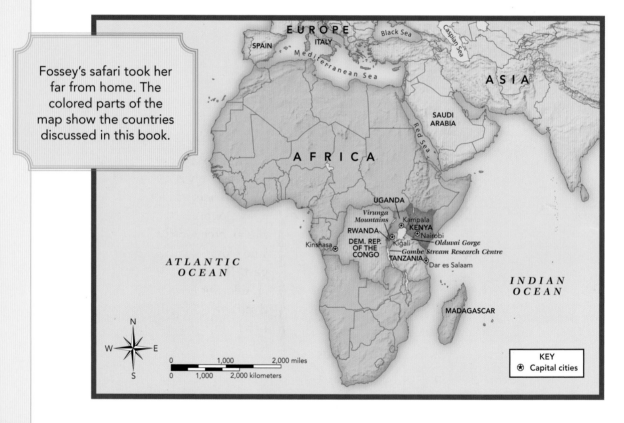

Fossey's safari took her far from home. The colored parts of the map show the countries discussed in this book.

She left on the trip of her dreams in September 1963. First she traveled to Tanzania in eastern Africa to visit Louis and Mary Leakey. The Leakeys were important scientists and naturalists. They studied **fossils**, or the remains of living things preserved in rock for millions of years. The fossils gave them information about early human ancestors who lived millions of years ago.

Louis and Mary Leakey pose with an early hominid skull, thought to be 600,000 years old! The discovery of this skull proved that humans lived far earlier than previously believed.

Meet the Leakeys

Dr. Louis S. B. Leakey (1903–1972) was a famous **anthropologist**. Anthropology is the study of human development and behavior. His wife, Mary Douglas Leakey (1913–1996), was an **archaeologist**. Archaeologists study fossils to learn about the past. The Leakeys worked together in Africa for many years. They discovered fossils of early **hominids**, or human ancestors, that lived as long as 25 million years ago.

A bad beginning

Fossey traveled to the Leakeys' work site at Olduvai Gorge in Tanzania. She was excited to meet her hero, Dr. Louis Leakey. He told her how important it was to study gorillas and other apes in their natural **habitat** in the wild.

While Fossey was at Olduvai, Dr. Leakey took her to see the latest fossil discovery. Excited, Fossey sprinted down a steep hillside toward the dig site, tripped, and broke her right ankle. The pain was terrible, and she was very embarrassed. One of the Leakeys' workers had to carry her out of the dig site on piggyback. It was not a good start for someone who wanted to be a naturalist.

Kabara meadow

Fossey's next stop was Kabara meadow, where she hoped to see mountain gorillas. Kabara is in a mountainous area in the Democratic Republic of Congo. The naturalist George Schaller had studied the mountain gorillas there in 1959 and 1960.

The trip up to the **remote** spot in the Virunga Mountains took five hours. The climb was especially difficult for Fossey, with her broken ankle. With the help of a cane, Fossey slowly climbed up to the meadow.

A gorilla **tracker** named Sanwekwe led Fossey's group through the dense forest. Sanwekwe had worked with Schaller and knew how to spot and follow mountain gorilla tracks.

Suddenly, after several hours of following gorilla tracks, Fossey smelled a strong scent. She later wrote that it was like a "barnyard" smell. Then the sound of screams and **chest-beats** burst through the quiet forest. Fossey and her group stood silent and still.

First glimpse of the gorillas

She peered through the trees and saw a group of gorillas about 50 feet (15 meters) away. The gorillas were peeking back at her! They seemed curious and nonthreatening. Their large black bodies looked striking against the deep green of the forest. She was in awe of the shy creatures and took many photographs of them. She knew then that she wanted to come back to Africa and study the mountain gorillas in the wild.

Great apes

Gorillas, chimpanzees, **bonobos**, and orangutans are known as the **great apes**. Great apes are large, tailless **primates**. Primates have humanlike features and large brains. The great apes live in the tropical forests of central and western Africa and Southeast Asia. Gorillas are the largest of the great apes. The only animals closer to humans are chimpanzees.

A mountain gorilla enjoys a quiet moment in the forest.

Back to Africa

After the trip, Fossey returned to her home and her job in Kentucky, dreaming of returning to Africa. In 1966 she took a giant step closer to that goal.

She read in the newspaper that **anthropologist** Dr. Louis Leakey was going to give a talk in Louisville, so she went to hear it. Afterward Fossey approached Dr. Leakey and reminded him of their meeting in Africa three years earlier. She eagerly showed him the articles she had written about the trip as well as photographs she had taken of the gorillas.

This lone gorilla is resting in the dense foliage of the Virunga Mountains.

Naturalist Jane Goodall and a baby chimpanzee reach out to touch each other's hands in Gombe Stream National Park, Tanzania.

Meet Jane Goodall

Before Dr. Leakey sent Fossey to Africa to study mountain gorillas, he set up a long-term field study of chimpanzees. In July 1960 he sent English naturalist Jane Goodall to Gombe Stream Research Center in Tanzania. Today, her work continues. The Jane Goodall Institute leads worldwide efforts to protect chimpanzees and their **habitat**.

Dr. Leakey was impressed. He told her he was about to set up a long-term **field study** of the mountain gorilla in central Africa. All he needed was the right researcher. He thought she might be the person he was looking for.

Dr. Leakey told Fossey to have her appendix taken out before moving to Africa. (The appendix is an organ. It is not necessary and can be removed without harming a person.) Living in a **remote** area far from hospitals could be dangerous, he explained. If her appendix became infected, she could die. So she should have it taken out before leaving, just in case.

Fossey had the operation, but later found out Dr. Leakey had been joking. He said it to test whether she was serious about going to Africa. He had an odd sense of humor!

Virunga Mountains

Fossey prepared for the move. She bought a *Teach Yourself Swahili* book to learn the local language. In December 1966 she left for Africa. It was hard for her to say goodbye to her young patients and to her three dogs—Brownie, Mitzi, and Shep. She had no idea how long she would be away.

Fossey landed in Nairobi, Kenya. There she spent time with wildlife photographers Joan and Alan Root. Joan Root helped Fossey buy supplies to set up her camp. Then naturalist Jane Goodall invited Fossey to visit. Fossey spent two days at Goodall's Gombe Stream Research Center. Goodall showed her how to organize camp and collect data on the apes.

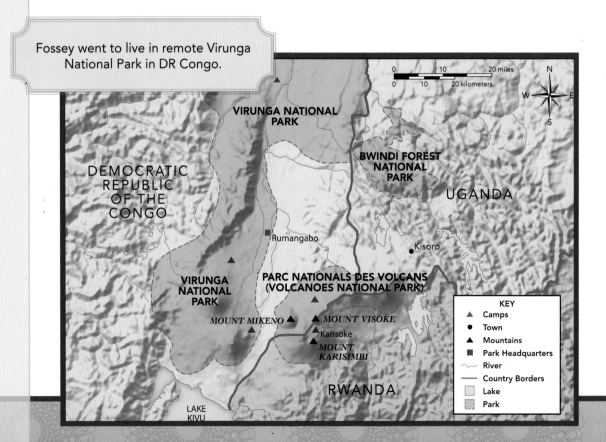

Fossey went to live in remote Virunga National Park in DR Congo.

Kabara meadow sits at a high point in the Virunga Mountains.

Then it was time to set up camp in the mountains of Virunga **National Park**. A national park is a protected area of land. Fossey bought an old Land Rover and named the car Lily. Then she started on the difficult, 700-mile (1,130-kilometer) drive from Kenya to the Democratic Republic of Congo. Alan Root made the journey with her.

Disappearing species

When Fossey went to Africa to study the mountain gorilla, fewer than 250 were left in the wild. The gorillas' habitat was shrinking because humans were taking over their land. About 40 percent of their protected park habitat was being used for farming.

On January 6, 1967, Dian Fossey, Alan Root, and two African workers made the trek up Mount Mikeno in the Virunga Mountains. Fossey was finally back at Kabara meadow!

Root stayed for two days, but then he had to leave. Loneliness hit Fossey hard. "I felt a sense of panic watching Alan fade into the **foliage**," Fossey wrote in *Gorillas in the Mist*. "I clung onto my tent pole simply to avoid running after him."

Camping at Kabara

Now Fossey was alone. The only humans on the mountain with her were two Africans who spoke only Swahili. Fossey tried to speak with them but found their language difficult. Somehow they were able to communicate, using hand gestures and a few words in each other's language.

Fossey's first task after Alan Root left was setting up camp. She put out barrels to collect rainwater, set up clotheslines for drying her gear, and showed her workers how to use the stove. Her house was a tent that was 10 by 7 feet (3 by 2 meters) in size. This tiny space served as her bedroom, office, living room, and bath! It housed crates containing all her supplies as well as file cabinets for keeping her field notes organized.

This was nothing like her home in Kentucky. Wild animals roamed all around. A few days after she arrived, an elephant rubbed against her tent and knocked her out of bed!

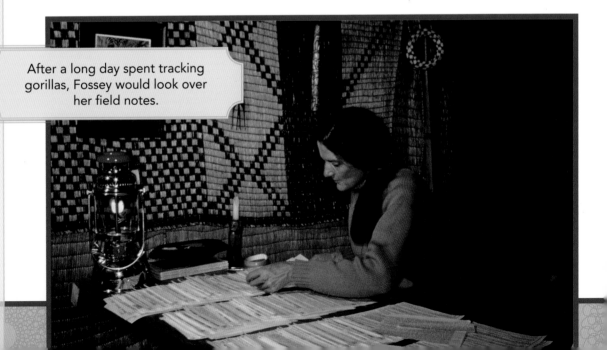

After a long day spent tracking gorillas, Fossey would look over her field notes.

First ape encounters

Fossey's first attempts at **tracking** in Kabara did not go very well. First, she scared away a male gorilla lounging in the sun. Then, she spent hours observing a large black animal on a slope, only to discover it was a giant forest hog!

Soon Sanwekwe, the **tracker** from her first trip, joined her at Kabara meadow. With his help, her tracking improved. She was able to get closer and closer to gorilla groups. She learned to recognize a few gorillas in each group and then assigned each group a number. She followed three groups around Kabara, taking careful notes about everything they did. The notes went something like this: "Group 3 spent two hours eating bamboo. At 3 p.m. the gorillas headed west."

A curious gorilla peers at Fossey through the foliage.

Getting to know the gorillas

Once a month Fossey drove two hours to the closest town, Kisoro, for supplies. She would stock up on goods such as powdered milk, vegetables, tuna, noodles, and oatmeal. Bread and cheese were hard to find, but a hen named Lucy gave plenty of eggs.

Locals helped Fossey get her supplies back to camp.

Fossey went tracking daily with Sanwekwe. She learned to tell the gorillas apart by their nose prints, or the pattern of their nostrils and the bridge of their nose. Just as humans have unique fingerprints, no two gorillas have the same nose print. Fossey peered at the gorillas through binoculars and sketched their nose prints.

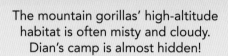

The mountain gorillas' high-altitude habitat is often misty and cloudy. Dian's camp is almost hidden!

Over time she was able to get closer to the gorillas. First she tried imitating their **chest-beats**. But soon she realized they saw these as a threat. So she tried imitating other gorilla movements, such as scratching and feeding. That seemed to work. She would crouch down in the foliage and imitate their movements and **vocalizations** (noises). After six months she could get as close as 30 feet (9 meters) from the gorillas.

Gorillas, gorillas, gorillas!

Fossey studied a **species** (type) of gorilla known as the mountain gorilla. Its Latin, or scientific, name is *Gorilla gorilla beringei*. Mountain gorillas have longer hair, shorter arms, and wider nostrils than lowland gorillas. Lowland gorillas are the type commonly found in zoos. Lowland gorillas are divided into two species: the western lowland gorilla (*Gorilla gorilla gorilla*) and the eastern lowland gorilla (*Gorilla gorilla graueri*).

Forced to leave

On July 9, 1967, Fossey received terrible news: A **civil war** had broken out in DR Congo. Soldiers told her she must leave camp at once for her own safety. The next day soldiers carried all her supplies down the mountain. They held her in Rumangabo, the park headquarters. She wondered, "Will I ever see my gorillas again?"

A New Start

Soldiers held Fossey in Rumangabo for two weeks. She knew she would have to escape. She convinced soldiers to let her cross the border to register her car, Lily. During the night she loaded Lily with her research notes, her cameras, and her hen, Lucy. Then, in the morning, two guards drove with her to the Rwandan border. At first the border guards would not let her through. She showed them her paperwork and argued with them for several hours. Finally, they allowed her to enter Rwanda.

As soon as she had crossed the border, she fled the soldiers and drove to the Traveler's Rest Hotel. She hid there under a bed until the Congolese soldiers were turned away. Now she could not return to DR Congo. They would arrest her as an escaped prisoner!

Fossey was sad she had to leave the mountain gorillas she had tracked for months.

Safe at last

So Fossey flew to Nairobi, Kenya, to meet up with Dr. Leakey. Dr. Leakey was pleased to see Fossey and relieved that she was safe. While she was being held prisoner in DR Congo, the U.S. government had declared her missing and thought dead! She was lucky to escape DR Congo.

Dr. Leakey persuaded Fossey to go back to the Virunga Mountains region and continue her valuable study of the mountain gorilla. But this time she would live on the other side of the mountain range, in Rwanda. It was just a few miles from her old camp at Kabara meadow, but she would be safe from the Congolese soldiers there. She could continue her research where she had left off. But 19 weeks had passed since she had seen a mountain gorilla. Would she be able to locate her gorillas again?

Once Fossey had returned to the Virunga Mountains, she was determined to continue studying the gorillas.

Karisoke

Fossey climbed up steep Mount Karisimbi to find a good spot for her new camp. Suddenly she spied a clearing in the mist. From there she could see the entire Virunga mountain range.

The spot was between Mount Karisimbi and Mount Visoke. So, Fossey named her new camp Karisoke—she made up the name by combining the "Kari" from Karisimbi and the "soke" from Visoke. Fossey lived at Karisoke in a small tent like the one she had at her old camp. She had very few comforts. There was not even hot running water.

Fossey and her workers built cabins and other structures to improve the camp.

Gorilla habitats

The Virunga mountain range is actually a chain of extinct volcanoes spanning about 50 miles (80 kilometers). Most of the area is covered with dense **vegetation** that thins out as one travels higher up into the mountains. Dotting the mountain range at higher **elevations** are meadows, such as the one where Fossey set up camp. Karisoke was located in the Parc National des Volcans, which means "Volcanoes **National Park**" in French. (French is one of the languages spoken in Rwanda.) This is a protected area of 30,000 acres (12,000 hectares) set aside for the gorillas.

The mountain gorillas' **habitat** is cloudy, misty, and cold. It is also at a high elevation, about 14,000 feet (4,270 meters) above sea level. This makes it difficult for many humans to live there. At very high elevations, the air has less oxygen, so it is harder to breathe.

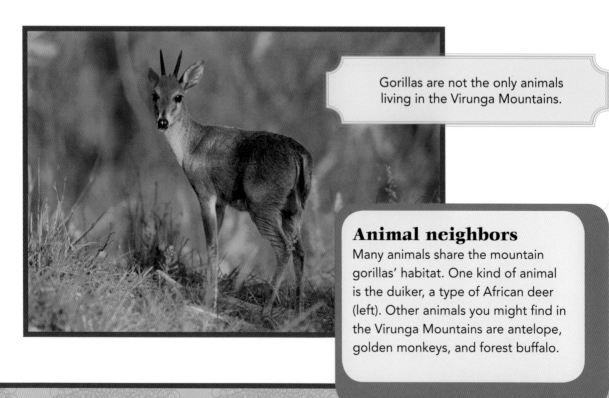

Gorillas are not the only animals living in the Virunga Mountains.

Animal neighbors

Many animals share the mountain gorillas' habitat. One kind of animal is the duiker, a type of African deer (left). Other animals you might find in the Virunga Mountains are antelope, golden monkeys, and forest buffalo.

Gorilla tracking

Fossey's **tracker** did not follow her to Rwanda. So she had to teach new workers how to **track** gorillas. One way is to look for bent vegetation. When gorillas pass through dense vegetation, it bends in the direction of their travel. You can also follow their knuckle prints. Gorillas get around by knuckle walking. They put most of their weight on their back limbs, pressing their front knuckles into the ground as they go. This leaves knuckle prints that point the way they are going. Another sign trackers look for is deposits of gorilla dung.

In her first year at Karisoke, Fossey tracked four groups—a total of 51 gorillas. She observed the same groups for years, noting every birth and death. She followed them daily as they traveled within their **range**. A range is an area of land in which a gorilla group lives. It is usually between 1 and 6 square miles (3 and 15 square kilometers) in size.

A dominant male shows off his silvery back.

Gorillas travel about one-third of a mile (half a kilometer) per day. They spend about 30 percent of their day traveling, 30 percent feeding, and 40 percent resting. We know this because of Fossey's research.

Gorilla groups

Gorilla groups can have between two and twenty members. Most have about ten. Groups have one **silverback**, which is a **mature** male over fifteen years old, weighing about 375 pounds (170 kilograms). It is the **dominant** gorilla, or the leader. Its name comes from the streak of white or silver hair on its back.

This young mountain gorilla hangs from a vine in the Bwindi forest, Uganda, while enjoying a leafy snack!

In addition, there are three or four mature females over eight years old, weighing about 200 pounds (90 kilograms) each. Next, there is a **blackback**, an **immature** male between eight and thirteen, weighing 250 pounds (115 kilograms). Groups usually have three to six other members—a combination of immature gorillas six to eight years old, juveniles three to six, and infants under three.

GENTLE GIANTS

Every day at Karisoke, Fossey spent time **tracking** and observing the gorillas. Slowly the gorillas became **habituated**. They grew used to being followed and observed by humans. The process of habituating gorillas can take months or even years. Over time the gorillas near Karisoke got to know Fossey and allowed her to observe them from nearby.

This way Fossey was able to learn a lot about gorilla behavior. She learned that the **silverback**, or oldest adult male, protects the group from danger. She also learned that gorillas communicate with one another in many ways—by making faces, by gesturing with their front limbs, and by making different **vocalizations**. These vocalizations range from loud screams, when frightened, to low, brief grunting sounds. Fossey called these sounds pig-grunts. Gorillas pig-grunt when they are happy or content.

Gorillas are herbivores, which means that they eat mostly plants.

Gorilla-size appetite
Adult mountain gorillas can eat as much as 60 pounds (27 kilograms) of vegetation a day!

Fossey tracked the gorillas through the mountains, noting their every movement. By day they travel and feed. Gorillas are mainly **herbivores**, eating the leaves and stems of plants such as celery, thistles, and nettles. They love bamboo and will dig eagerly in the earth to get at the tender shoots. They also occasionally eat worms or grubs and some fruits such as wild blackberries. At night mountain gorillas build nests in which to sleep. They bend long stalks of **foliage**, tucking in the leafy ends. This forms a soft patch of **vegetation** shaped like a shallow bathtub. Sometimes they make nests in hollow tree trunks.

Gorillas are nothing like the fierce creatures shown in the movies, Fossey learned. They are not likely to attack humans or other animals unless they feel threatened. Instead, gorillas are social creatures with close-knit family groups. Fossey called them "gentle giants!"

Movies such as *King Kong* portrayed gorillas as fierce monsters.

Captured on film

In 1968 *National Geographic* magazine sent photographer Bob Campbell to take pictures of Fossey and her gentle giants. Through 1972 he made several visits to Karisoke, often for months at a time. He went on tracking trips with Fossey and took roll after roll of photos of the shy mountain gorillas. He also helped out at camp by building cabins, training the Rwandan staff, and doing **census** work. A census is a count of how many gorillas are left in an area. Sadly, the number of mountain gorillas in the Virunga Mountains had gone down since naturalist George Schaller had done his census in 1960.

In 1969 Campbell caught an amazing moment on film. Fossey was crouched in the foliage, imitating gorilla pig-grunts and pretending to eat shoots. Slowly a young male gorilla named Peanuts lumbered over to her. Then he reached out and touched her hand! It was the first peaceful contact between humans and gorillas in the wild ever captured on film. No one knew whether this had ever happened before.

Fossey gained the gorillas' trust by imitating their movements. In this photograph she scratches, just like Peanuts.

A baby mountain gorilla shows affection toward an adult.

The photos made Fossey famous. The National Geographic Society agreed to fund her research and put her on the cover of the *National Geographic* magazine. Now everyone knew of Dian Fossey and her mountain gorillas!

National Geographic

The National Geographic Society was founded in 1888 in Washington, DC, to spread knowledge of geography, or Earth's features. The society has funded many projects and studies, including Jane Goodall's and Dian Fossey's work with **great apes**. The society puts out a widely read magazine, *National Geographic*. Today the group has over nine million members. It is the world's largest scientific society.

GORILLAS IN DANGER

Fossey's 1970s **census** showed that the mountain gorilla population was shrinking fast. In 1960 George Schaller had estimated there were about 450 gorillas in the Virunga Mountains region. Now there were fewer than 250. Fossey worried that the mountain gorilla might become extinct.

Virunga-area gorillas faced many dangers. One was farmers moving into their **habitat** to graze cattle. The farmers and cattle scared away the gorillas and trampled the **vegetation** they ate.

Poaching problem

A worse problem was **poachers**. Poachers illegally move into protected areas and steal or kill wild animals. Most poachers around Karisoke were not interested in gorillas. Instead, they hunted bushbuck (a type of small, striped antelope) and duikers for food. But their traps could not tell the difference between a duiker and a gorilla. The sharp wire often snared gorillas, causing horrible injuries to their wrists and ankles. Some gorillas died from these injuries.

Habituated mountain gorillas enjoy close contact with Fossey.

Other poachers went after gorillas directly. Some trapped gorillas to sell to zoos in Europe and the United States. The problem was that it was almost impossible to safely trap just one gorilla. Many gorillas received serious injuries during capture. Sick or starving, captive gorillas usually died before they made it out of Africa.

Sometimes an attempt to capture one gorilla would result in the injury, or even death, of an entire group. Adult gorillas fight fiercely to protect their young. Poachers often had to slaughter an entire gorilla group just to capture one **immature** gorilla for a zoo.

A small number of poachers killed gorillas to sell their body parts as **souvenirs**. People bought objects like gorilla skulls or ashtrays made from gorilla hands! This cruel practice made Fossey furious.

But Fossey faced a huge battle. There were only 12 park guards for the entire 30,000-acre Volcanoes National Park. What could one person do?

Gruesome collections like these gorilla skulls angered Fossey.

In this aerial photograph the boundary between Virunga National Park and the land used by local farmers is clear.

Fighting back

The mountain gorillas were in danger of becoming extinct. So Fossey vowed to do everything she could to protect them.

First, she asked the cattle farmers to graze their herds outside the park. If they did not listen, she drove away their cattle. She also led camp staff on **patrols** to drive away poachers. She got rid of their animal traps and threw away the belongings they stored in the forest.

What's in a name?

The word *Visoke* means "a place where the herds are watered." Farmers had taken cattle to drink at Ngezi Lake on Mount Visoke for over 400 years. Fossey said it was hard to tell the farmers not to use the land their people had used for centuries. Still, she felt she had to protect the land for the gorillas.

She used more extreme measures to drive away poachers who attacked gorillas. Some poachers hunted gorillas out of a belief in *sumu*, or magic. Poachers would kill **silverbacks** for their ears, tongues, or small fingers and then make a brew with the parts. They believed drinking this brew made them strong like a silverback. So Fossey tried to convince them she had powerful *sumu* as well.

Once Fossey caught a ten-year-old boy hiding in the **foliage** with a bow and arrow. He was the son of a leading poacher, Munyarukiko. She took the boy back to Karisoke and held him there for two days. Munyarukiko got his boy back after he promised not to hunt or trap in the area again.

Fossey called her **tactics** active **conservation** (protection). Some people thought she went too far. But she was desperate to protect the mountain gorilla from dying out and was willing to do so at all costs.

Fossey fought to protect the remaining mountain gorillas from poaching and illegal farming.

Digit was Fossey's favorite mountain gorilla. She met him on her first day at camp in Rwanda.

Death of Digit

By 1970 Fossey had spent thousands of hours **tracking** and observing mountain gorillas in the wild. Now it was time to share what she had learned with other scientists and naturalists.

Fossey left Africa that year to study at the University of Cambridge in England. She gathered all her field notes from Kabara and Karisoke for a long paper titled "The Behavior of the Mountain Gorilla." In 1974 Cambridge awarded her a doctoral degree in **zoology**, or the study of animals, for her work.

Return to Africa

Later that year she returned to Rwanda to continue her research. She took several students with her. Karisoke was now drawing students and researchers from the United States and Great Britain to study the rare mountain gorilla.

In early January 1978, a **tracker** returned to Karisoke with terrible news about Group 4, one of the gorilla groups Fossey was studying. He had followed their trail into the forest, only to find poacher tracks and blood. The next day Fossey and several others set out at dawn to find Group 4. On the trail they discovered Fossey's favorite gorilla, Digit, hacked apart on the ground. His head and hands were missing. Digit had died defending his group from six poachers.

Fossey was extremely upset. She felt like someone had killed a close friend or family member. She brought Digit's body back to Karisoke and buried him close to her cabin.

Television programs in the United States shared news of Digit's murder. Hundreds of thousands of people saw pictures of Digit in the pages of *National Geographic*. Now many mourned the loss of this gentle mountain gorilla.

Remembering Digit
Fossey started the Digit Fund to bring worldwide attention to protecting mountain gorillas. Today it is called the Dian Fossey Gorilla Fund International.

Fossey writes a gorilla's name on its grave marker.

Final years at Karisoke

Digit's death strongly affected Fossey. Afterward, she increased her conservation efforts. She spoke out against tourists visiting the gorillas in the Virunga Mountains. She thought they would disturb the gorillas' peaceful habitat and perhaps even bring disease.

She also declared war on poaching. She increased the number of poaching patrols and went to great lengths to drive away poachers, sometimes using a gun to scare them off. Her actions angered many local park officials. Some students and researchers at Karisoke disagreed with things Fossey did.

Fossey organized groups of armed guards to patrol the national park.

By 1979 her backers at the National Geographic Society were alarmed by her tactics. So they convinced her to take a three-year leave, or break, from studying the gorillas.

The next year Fossey returned to the United States. She became a professor at Cornell University in Ithaca, New York. While teaching there, she completed her famous book, *Gorillas in the Mist*. It was named for the misty, high-**elevation** habitat of the mountain gorillas. She also wrote articles on the gorillas' behavior, diet, and habitat.

Back to the gorillas

In 1983 Fossey returned to her home among the mountain gorillas. Her health was fading. She had trouble breathing and did not have the energy she used to. Still, she carried out her gorilla observations and continued her fight against poachers.

Fossey was buried next to the gorillas she had tried to save. Her gravestone is at the top right of this photograph.

On December 26, 1985, she lost the battle. The next morning camp staff found her dead body in the cabin. She had been killed with a *panga*, a type of large knife used by local poachers. Many blamed poachers for her murder. Others thought it might have been a Rwandan park official, upset that Fossey spoke out against tourism, which brought the park money. Whatever the cause, Fossey died among the mountain gorillas she had fought so hard to protect.

Her Work Goes On

Dian Fossey put her life at risk to protect the mountain gorillas. In the end she gave her life for them. Her gravestone at Karisoke reads: "No one loved gorillas more."

Some may not have liked Fossey's active **conservation tactics**. But her efforts to save the mountain gorilla worked. A **census** taken four years after her death showed a growing number of gorillas around Karisoke.

Today there are about 380 gorillas in the Virunga Mountains, where Fossey did her research, and about 320 in the Bwindi forest in Uganda. However, the **species** is still very much at risk. The mountain gorilla is critically **endangered** and may die out soon.

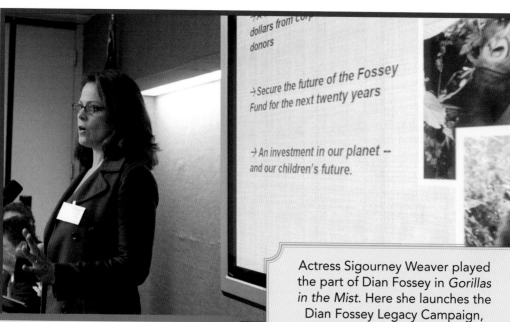

Gorillas on the big screen
A movie about Dian Fossey's life called *Gorillas in the Mist* came out in 1988.

Actress Sigourney Weaver played the part of Dian Fossey in *Gorillas in the Mist*. Here she launches the Dian Fossey Legacy Campaign, which raises money for African conservation programs, including the Karisoke Research Center.

Doomed gorillas?

Even lowland gorillas, once large in number, struggle to survive. Only 35,000 western lowland gorillas remain. About 60 percent of the species has died out within the past 25 years. War in central Africa has destroyed some of the gorillas' **habitat**. Other gorillas have died from diseases spread by humans, such as the deadly Ebola virus. Scientists estimate that within 50 years all wild **great apes** will be extinct.

The world may lose Fossey's gentle giants forever. What would Dian Fossey do if she were alive today? What can you do?

New zoos

Fossey did not believe that keeping gorillas captive was a good way to protect the species. But if there had to be zoos, she thought they should try to imitate the gorillas' natural habitat. Instead of bars and cages, Fossey pushed for open enclosures with water, trees, **foliage**, and hidden food. This type of habitat is common today at zoos like the Brookfield Zoo in Chicago and the London Zoo.

Dian Fossey shares a peaceful moment with the mountain gorillas she was fighting to protect.

TIMELINES

Dian Fossey's life

1932   Born in San Francisco, California, on January 16.

1949   Graduates from Lowell High School.

1954   Graduates from San Jose State with a degree in **occupational therapy**.

1955   Moves to Louisville, Kentucky.

1963   Travels to Africa on **safari**.

1966   Moves to Democratic Republic of Congo to study mountain gorillas.

1967   **Civil war** breaks out in DR Congo; Fossey sets up a new camp in Volcanoes **National Park** in Rwanda.

1968   National Geographic Society sends photographer Bob Campbell to Virunga Mountains.

1969   Campbell captures on film the first peaceful contact between humans and gorillas in the wild.

1974   University of Cambridge, in England, awards Fossey a doctoral degree in **zoology**.

1977   Fossey's favorite gorilla, Digit, dies. He was killed by **poachers**.

1980   Fossey moves to New York to teach at Cornell University; completes book *Gorillas in the Mist*.

1983   Returns to Karisoke in Rwanda.

1985   Killed on December 26.

World timeline

1758   Swedish naturalist Carl Linnaeus describes a group of animals he calls **primates**, which includes humans and **great apes**.

1888   National Geographic Society founded in Washington, DC.

1959–1960   George Schaller studies mountain gorillas in Virunga Mountains. The first official **census** shows 450 mountain gorillas in the area.

1960   Jane Goodall travels to Tanzania to study chimpanzees at Gombe Stream Research Center.

1970s   Census shows mountain gorilla population shrinking, with only about 240 gorillas in Virunga Mountains area.

1979   Mountain Gorilla Project founded to support gorilla **conservation**.

2003   Census shows mountain gorilla population in Volcanoes National Park has grown to about 380; population of mountain gorillas in Uganda's Bwindi forest is about 320.

2007   Lowland gorilla population shrinking; all gorilla **species** now critically **endangered**.

GLOSSARY

anthropologist person who studies human development and behavior

archaeologist person who studies fossils to learn about the past

blackback male gorilla between eight and thirteen years old. Each mountain gorilla group has one blackback.

bonobo type of ape that looks similar to a chimpanzee, with longer limbs and a more slender body. Bonobos live in a small region of Africa, south of the Congo River.

census count of the number of something in an area

chest-beat sound an adult male gorilla makes by rapidly pounding his chest. They do this when they are excited or alarmed.

civil war war between two groups within the same country

conservation act of protecting or preserving natural resources

disabled impaired. Fossey helped disabled children at Kosair Children's Hospital in Louisville, Kentucky.

dominant most powerful or in control; the leader. The dominant male gorilla is the silverback.

ecology branch of science dealing with living things and their environment. Pollution harms the ecology of Earth.

elevation how high something is above sea-level. Fossey built her camp, Karisoke, at a high elevation.

endangered in danger of dying out. Mountain gorillas are critically endangered.

field study research undertaken where something lives or takes place. Dr. Louis Leakey sent Fossey and Jane Goodall on long-term field studies.

foliage cluster of leaves, flowers, and branches. Fossey hid in the foliage to observe gorillas without frightening them.

fossil remains of a living thing preserved in rock or soil. Fossils tell us when certain plants and animals lived on Earth.

great ape group of animals that includes the gorilla, orangutan, chimpanzee, and bonobo. Great apes are in danger of becoming extinct.

habitat where a living thing lives. The gorillas' habitat is shrinking.

habituate become used to the presence of humans. It takes months or years to habituate mountain gorillas.

herbivore plant eater. Mountain gorillas are mostly herbivores.

hominid group that includes humans and human ancestors

immature not fully grown or developed. Gorilla groups usually contain four to six immature gorillas.

mature fully grown or developed. Mature female gorillas are over eight years old.

national park protected area of land, usually set aside by the government. National parks are important places to preserve living things.

occupational therapy job of helping sick and injured people relearn daily tasks such as dressing, eating, and performing a job. Fossey worked as an occupational therapist early in her career.

patrol regular tour of a place to keep guard. Fossey organized regular patrols to keep her gorillas safe from illegal hunters.

poacher illegal hunter. Mountain gorillas are in danger from poachers.

primate group of mammals (hairy animals that feed milk to their young) with good vision, large brains, and grasping limbs

range area in which a gorilla group travels. Mountain gorillas' ranges are between 1 and 6 square miles (3 and 15 square kilometers) in size.

remote far away or hard to reach. Fossey spent years living in a remote area in Africa.

safari journey for the purpose of observing wild animals up close. Fossey planned a safari in Africa.

silverback oldest male gorilla in a group over 15 years old. Silverbacks weigh about 375 pounds (170 kilograms) and have a streak of white or silver hair on their back.

souvenir object that serves as a reminder of a place or person

species group of animals with the same characteristics that can mate together and produce offspring. There are two main species of gorillas—the lowland gorilla and the mountain gorilla.

tactic way of doing something

track follow a path made by an animal's tracks

tracker person who follows a path made by an animal's tracks. Fossey relied on a skilled tracker named Sanwekwe to find mountain gorillas in DR Congo.

vegetation plant life. The Virunga Mountains are covered with dense vegetation.

veterinarian doctor who treats animals. Fossey's love of animals made her want to be a veterinarian.

vocalization noise made by an animal. One type of gorilla vocalization is the pig-grunt.

zoology study of animals. Fossey received a doctoral degree in zoology.

Want to Know More?

Books

Kalman, Bobbie, and Kristina Lundblad. *Endangered Mountain Gorillas (Earth's Endangered Animals)*. New York: Crabtree, 2004.

Simon, Seymour. *Gorillas*. New York: HarperCollins, 2003.

Taylor, Marianne. *Mountain Gorilla (Animals Under Threat)*. Chicago: Heinemann Library, 2004.

Websites

www.gorillafund.org
Visit the website of the Dian Fossey Gorilla Fund International to read more about Fossey's work and to learn how her research lives on.

www.awf.org/content/wildlife/detail/mountaingorilla
Visit the African Wildlife Foundation to learn more about threats to the mountain gorilla and what the foundation is doing to save it.

http://kids.nationalgeographic.com/Animals/CreatureFeature/Mountain-gorilla
Visit *National Geographic's* website to learn fun facts about mountain gorillas, see pictures and videos of gorillas in action, and listen to the gorillas' vocalizations.

Places to visit

Smithsonian National Zoo
3001 Connecticut Avenue NW • Washington, DC 20008 • (202) 633-4800
http://nationalzoo.si.edu
See mountain gorillas' closest cousins, western lowland gorillas, up close at the National Zoo. Visitors, with a parent's help, can adopt a western lowland gorilla by giving money to support its care at the zoo.

Natural History Museum, London
Cromwell Road • London SW7 5BD • United Kingdom • +44 (0)20 7942 5000
www.nhm.ac.uk
Visit the Mammal Balcony and view a life-size model of a mountain gorilla.

INDEX